Sort of Made in Brooklyn

Sharon Eustaquio

BookLeaf
Publishing

India | USA | UK

Presentation by *BookLeaf Publishing*

Web: www.bookleafpub.com

E-mail: info@bookleafpub.com

ISBN: 9789358318197

First edition 2023

ACKNOWLEDGEMENT

Para mis padres, Irene & Rafael, por enseñarme a ser honesta, cariñosa, y valiente. Los quiero mucho.

A warm thank you to Lisa Ortiz, Mark Awai, and Catherine Lau, for overextending your kindness and helping me reach the end of this project.

PREFACE

How do you compose the notes of your broken heart into a ballad that isn't completely disagreeable? The answer is quite simple. You don't. You write about the moments that led to the heartbreak. You write about yourself and the people around you, because the story that unfolded wasn't just about one person. And then, somewhere in those chapters as you write, you also reflect. You step into the shoes of others, and look at your own character, your own person, and hopefully you come out the other end of the tunnel realizing what I did; That somewhere in those once lived dark moments, there was beauty there, too.

Por Amor

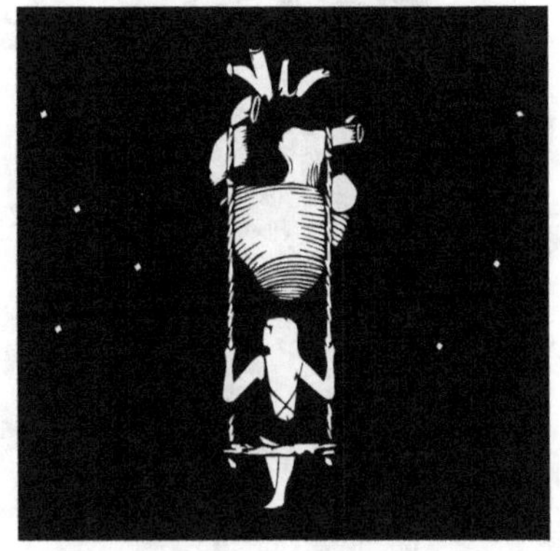

I think everyone has a little bit of crazy in them,
but sometimes we realize
that we can choose what to be crazy about.
I choose love.
I choose to live a life crazy for love.

Rosa

Más bella que una flor
Más fuerte que el sol en los días más caliente del verano
Raíces más fuertes que los árboles
Y una riza que iluminaba todos los cuartos que entraba.

Así era mi tía
Siempre demostrando ser más valiente que una guerrera
Era toda una luchadora
Y a la misma vez
Siempre compartiendo su corazón con toda la familia
Uniéndonos con solo su presencia.

Mi tía,
Nunca olvidaré sus rezos
Llenos de fe, humildad y cariño,
Ni sus abrazos, o su sonrisa
Pero más que nada
Nunca olvidare el amor que nos daba
Es el amor que vivirá con nosotros
Hasta que nos volvamos a ver
Mi tía querida, Mi tía Rosa.

Positivity Over Everything

I don't speak about grief often,
Not with family or friends.
They say it gets better with time.
But they're wrong.
Each passing hurts exactly like the first one.

It hurts even more when you didn't know them,
But you dreamt of meeting them.
Of learning their smile.
Their laughter.
Their scent.
You rely on the stories your folks tell about them,
Just to imagine a world that could have been.

My parents came here to give my brother and I a better life.
They sold their lives to a country that rejects them like a bad artery.
They pushed through the bad.
And were often greeted with more bad.
Yet you'll always see happiness on their face,
Which is why I'll always live a life that suffices,
All that they've endured.

UnDACAmented

Struggling to breathe;
What else is new?
These small lungs were not trained to carry all this cold air.

Flying on a prototype;
Maybe I'll land and find my stolen family,
But can I really fight against the currents,
Of our beloved Rio Bravo?

The media world drowns me.
Some claim they want to know how we are doing.
How we are feeling.
They want to feel our numbness.
Our fear.
But really, all they want,
Is to see us break,
Under the strokes of their negligent pens.

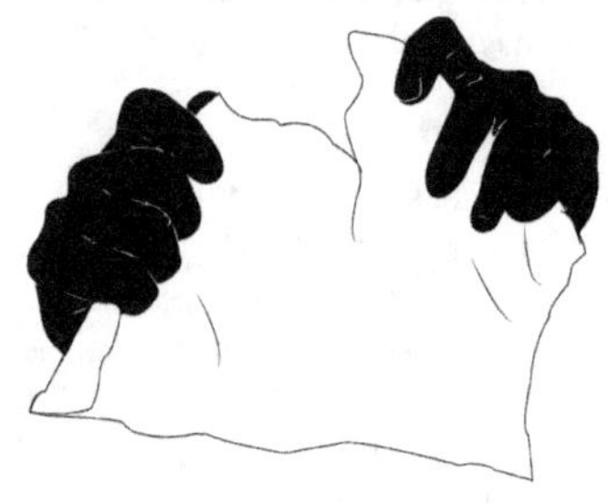

Legally Present

The weight that had been pressing down on my chest,
Keeping me from breathing,
Disappeared.
Just like that,
The air is thinner,
Crisper,
And my soul is happy.
I am home.

Guinea Pigs

When I was undocumented,
I believed that the hardest thing I'd ever experience
Is living without an identity,
Or humbly accepting the fate of being constantly disrespected
By strangers in the media
Who couldn't dare to bother seeing my human.

I'd grown so comfortable living in the unknown.
Or through the names of others.
I never questioned the lack of rage
In my father's eyes
Whenever cops questioned him
For crimes he would never dare to commit.
And it didn't seem strange
That my mother seemed content
With the opportunity to clean houses
That our family should never dream of owning,
While her own diplomas gathered dust
In a country we could never return to.

But I was wrong.
Because once America gave weight to my name,
And tried to cloth me with their delusional hopes of justice,
They forgot to disguise their guilt,
Which sat with me as I turned back to see,
My parents and my brother,
Dawdle in the distance.

Delusional Desires

Take your pupils off my chest
I beg you
Give my nerves a rest.

To be wanted by so many
Usually leads to
Being disrespected by plenty.

I don't want your entitled praises
Better yet
Keep me out of your misguided phases.

Can't you hear the scream in my brain
Telling you

There's nothing here for you to gain?

I just want my savant to be read
Without watching
The disgusting thoughts form in your head.

It's no wonder my eyes read of thunder
Come any closer
And I might commit a serious blunder.

Blocked

I cannot get past this wall.
Should I go over it?
Around?
Under it?

I am told when you're stuck
You should just keep going,
Even though that is totally contradictory.
"La vida te pondrá obstáculos,
Pero los límites los pones tú."

Nothing I tried worked.
So instead, I changed my direction.
Only to find myself coming back,
To the same damn barrier,
Every.
Single.
Time.

Until finally,
I reached a corner where I couldn't be seen,
Or heard.
El mundo siguió girando,
While I laid down and refused to watch.

Until they found me.
237 pairs of ojitos,
Asking me for help.

Me.
The person that was constantly tripping
Over visible items directly in front of her.

I blinked a few times,
Unsure if I saw the same despair in their eyes,
That I'd seen in my own reflection,
Or if I just yearned to belong.

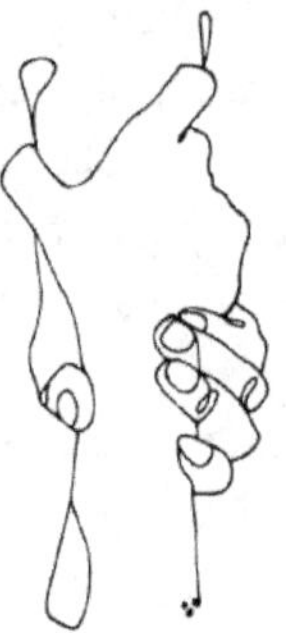

One by one they pulled me towards them,
Until we collectively arrived back at the same divide.
Instinctively, we forged our arms into a ladder.
Watching each other move forward,
Strengthened our resolve.

Until finally it was my turn,
I looked back at the team that'd saved me,
Not wanting to leave them behind.
Together they reassured me.
Ya era tiempo.

I took a deep breath,
And took the leap.
Promising myself I'd come back to build a bridge,
Or find a new squad to help me
Come knock the whole fucking thing down.

Fourteen Wildfires

I believed in the lyrics of our song.
They echoed through my lungs,
And my extremities,
Made me sway like the trees in the Fall,
When our love was always reborn,
Only to dry out by Spring.
Our love never made sense you see,
It paved many paths that made others wonder,
What we could be.
But our kindred souls knew
We didn't need anyone to hold our own.
But somewhere in the depths of the forests,
We lost ourselves.
Unable to find you was where I fell.
I called your name through the rivers,
Where I struggled to swim.
Until my voice disappeared for a while;
That was when I realized,
I couldn't live without singing.

Twin Tornadoes

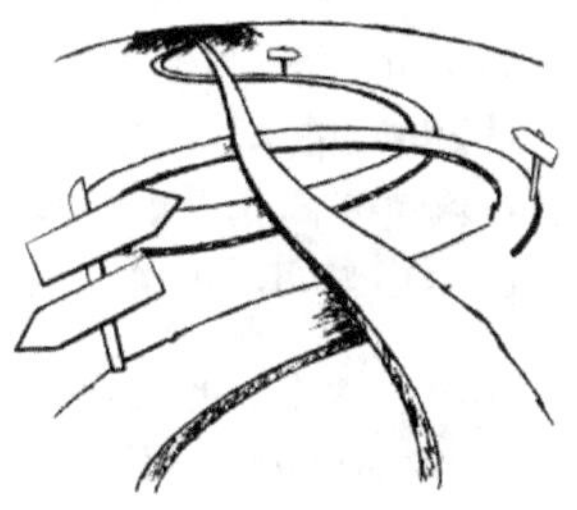

You moved twice this year.
There was neither enthusiasm,
Nor elation,
During either of those events.
It was so obvious that we were both scared to let go,
Even though we just didn't make sense anymore.
Time had changed us.
The distance between us could no longer be quantified,
No matter how many hours were spent trying.
Tired of separating our amalgamated belongings,
You never bothered to add your name to the lease,
And I never offered you the spare keys.
As you taped your boxes shut,
I watched from a distance,
Wondering when you wrapped up your heart,
Or if you ever unpacked it at all.

Earthquake

You knew my favorite birdsong
Happening at dawn
When the sun's rays permeated the dense stratosphere
Of our small studio apartment.

You'd always wake up bothered,
Bringing down the blinds,
Ceasing my hope for a better morning,
And simultaneously eulogizing your ego.

I missed all the exit signs
On this journey towards the white picket fence
That I would never encounter.
They were thickly veiled by my genuine alacrity.

You circumvented all your vows as a partner,
Yet still I was deluded.
Entranced by the potential
Of a home we would forget to scaffold.

It's no wonder why I'd soon ascend indifferent,
Perturbed by our whole relationship.
While you massaged your invariable habits,
My severed heart gradually absconded.

Famine

I stopped eating.
It helps distract me from all the pain
That's sinking my heavy heart.
My pericardium layers are severed.
My diaphragm's no longer intact.

I can't sleep either.
I want to run back to you,
But energy is what I lack.

It's a terrible feeling
Of wanting to go home
And not being able to.

I didn't even realize I was recreating it,
The very same scene,
Over and over,
Wanting home
But allowing situations that kept me away.

Now I have lost you,
My vessel is emptied,
Perhaps never to be filled again.

The Tunguska Meteorite

My heart hurts,
At the mere thought of what you're putting me through again.
It's not a refreshing surprise,
But rather one that I resent,
Because I can only blame myself,
For keeping that door open for you,
When I should have sealed it up,
And thrown away the key.

I thought I was done with the crying.
"There's no way he can hurt me again."
I lie to myself so easily when it comes to you.

Well there's a mirror at my bedside now,
And the truth can no longer hide,
In the clutter of your outdated habits.
For I have learned to take out the trash
Before it overflows into other organs.

I will no longer tolerate being belittled.
With my blood pumping through my veins,
I know I am stronger now than ever,
To release you,
And any tension my body holds,
In remembrance of you.

Exhalando

Last night I ran into you in the middle of Mexico,

On a dirt covered road,

In an area surrounded by mountains.

You spoke to me without the anger,

That's been hanging over your head,

For the past 10 months.

You even asked me to put you to sleep,

A gesture that stopped my heart in its tracks,

And made me turn to look at you.

It was really you,

Standing there with the smug look that I hate,

But can't seem to forget.

Infinitamente

I would do it again.

I would rebuild the entirety of the Roman Empire.

To see the shimmering that the sunlight brought,

And feel the rush of the city just once more.

I would do it again.

Even if it meant watching it fall once more.

Vivire Soñando

You came to me again last night,

In some strange straw-hat form.

It wasn't you,

But your face and voice were the same.

My family and I hid in a building,

That was quite viciously under attack.

As we heard your steps get closer,

I felt the sweat fall from my mom's back,

Onto my lap while she prayed for mercy.

My heart jumped when I saw you,

Unsure at first of your intentions,

Until you smiled,

And I instantly rose to embrace you.

You explained to us the escape route,

Which you had carefully planned out before deciding to barge in here.

Your arms had weapons surgically attached to them;

'What the hell happened to you?' I wondered.

As you led us down the hall,

Taking down anything or anyone that dared threaten us,

I remembered,

That feeling you used to give me,

Of being safe.

I watched in admiration as you led us out of harms away,

And I woke up wondering,

If you'd ever be that person for us,

Ever again.

Sheer Cupidity

I still think about that night
When you surprised me at work
And didn't even bother to turn off the lights
I can still feel your lips on the back of my neck
Your hands going up my thighs
Giving me goosebumps without even a peck

My heartbeat quickens in the contemplation of you
Ripping my stockings
Losing all control but not missing a single queue
Or a single button
Hearing my body and all of its waves
You gave me everything I could ever crave

We were completely sober
And yet my senses remain intoxicated by your devotion
We left my desk a mess that night
Papers scattered everywhere
Forgot entirely about the world or where we were
If it weren't for that facilities manager
We almost avoided a terrible plight.

Love in Tan Boots

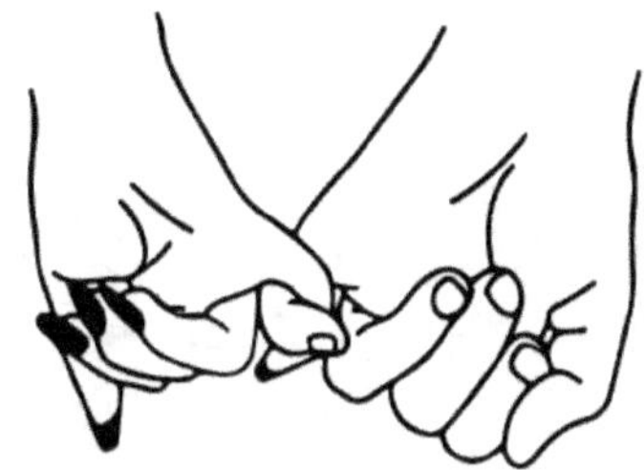

Our rhythm was never paced nor timid,
It was leveled,
Exhilarating,
Bold,
And very much difficult to camouflage.

Our cadence could be heard for miles,
Enthralling the thoughts of our audience.
Leaving them curious,
We didn't stop to amuse them.
In fact, we often forgot to notice them.

Our tactics were always misunderstood,
By others and by one another,
The presence of doubt loomed over our heads,
As our sweat meshed with my sheets,
And our passion fractured where I retire.

Nearing the moment where our time-lapse would end,
our pulse remained steady.
An honorable discharge seemed to be the only exit,
To the melancholic separation,
Of two souls that may frequent again.

Insatiate

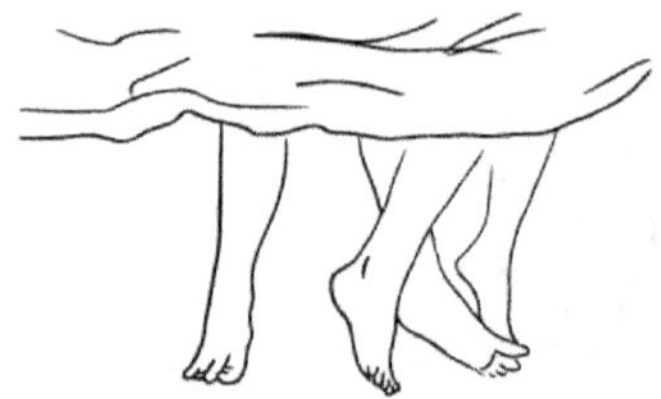

I want you to show up on my doorstep,
On a day where the rain is running through the city's veins,
washing away the sins of mankind,
Kiss me like you know me from another time,
Make us both forget that our passion is considered a crime.

I want to see your eyes under the moon,
Study your lips through the monsoon,
I want to feel your whisper in my ear,
And the heat steaming off your chest,
Until the sun crests through the shades far too soon.

Disclose the side of you that you're too afraid to share,
I'll hold you down because life isn't fair,
Teach you not to be scared,
Those moments are fleeting,
But our connection is so intense it changes the air.

Show me your fervor,
Take my fingers in your hand,
Sway my hips like I know you can,
But pace yourself,
What no one knows can be so divine,
We'll run out the clock on nobody's dime.

Serenidad

Your laughter
Brought a stillness to my ripple.
It was a calm I hadn't experienced
In many decades.

Every submerged moment we shared
Held a buoyancy
That could illuminate
The densest places in the universe.

Feeling secure
Is so frequently diluted
That I didn't even recognize the gesture
Until you were no longer within reach.

Without an intent
You raised my standards
For what I accept from those
Who sail in my direction.

As I sit here,
Watching the waves roll further away,
I know the warmth of your dawn
Will follow me through every existence.

Alas Sin Lagrimas

Un día vi un lirio de los valles
Floreciendo
En las grietas del pavimento
Fue en la misma temporada
Adonde reconocí
Todos los colores
De mi propio valor.

Pasaron varios años
Antes de poder recuperar mis fuerzas
Pero cuando renacieron
Se mantuvieron más firmes
Que la estatua de la libertad
Aguantando un huracán de desengaños.

Ahora las salas se detienen
Cuando escuchan mi voz inquebrantable
señalando hábitos
Que deben ser deshechos.
Tampoco ya nadie duda mis sueños
De sanar los corazones heridos
Y hacerlos creer de nuevo
Que mientras nos mantengamos unidos
Las estrellas al alcanzo se mantienen.

Ahora finalmente celebrare
El poder de volver a volar
Sin las cadenas que me envolvían
Y podré sembrar nuevas raíces
En las montañas más altas sin luces
Donde la comunidad mía
Por fin llevare.